HEDGEHOGG UNLEASHED

BY

ROB EDWARDS

ILLUSTRATIONS AND COVER ART

BY

ZOE EDWARDS

Email: robedwards378@gmail.com
Instagram: @hedgehogg_the_poet
Instagram: @sonnet.the.hedgehogg
TikTok: @hedgehogg_the_poet

Disclaimer
HEDGEHOGG UNLEASHED

Author: Rob Edwards
Instagram: @hedgehogg_the_poet
@sonnet.the.hedgehogg
robedwards378@gmail.com

Illustrations & Cover art by Zoe Edwards

Copyright © 2024 Rob Edwards

All rights reserved.
No part of this publication may be reproduced,
stored in
A retrieval system, or transmitted,
 in any form or by any
Means (electronic, mechanical,
 photocopying, recording
Or otherwise),
without the prior written permission of the
Publisher, except in the case of brief quotations
Embodied in critical reviews and other noncommercial
Uses permitted by Copyright Law.
ISBN: 9798884442573
Imprint: Independently published

Dedication

I dedicate this book to my beautiful supportive wife Cath.

You lit up the stars for me.

Beguiled

C rave to cwtch you in my welcoming mind.
A re shared secrets sure in the beginning?
T ender touching rhymes I will leave behind.
H air once long, for lush years has been thinning.
E ach day we find a moment to connect.
R outes through the darkness we seek out and find.
I n touch, our two minds meld and intersect.
N ever alone, our fates are intertwined.
E very day I'm once again beguiled.

Foreword

As a collector of words, I crave those that elicit emotions. Whether they are joyful or painful, melancholic and reflective, pure, complex or funny as hell, I want to feel them all.

As a mystery author, I tend to dabble in the darker recesses of the mind, but I don't linger there too long. I seek out the light, I walk that balance, and so, when I discovered the work of Rob Edwards, it felt like a gift.

This is how I came to hold both The Naked Hedgehogg and now, Hedgehogg Unleashed in my hands and why I'm honoured to call Rob Edwards's friend and to write these words today.

Seeking words that I needed to hear but not sure what they were, I uncovered Rob's unmistakable Welsh timbre one afternoon on my feed. Out in nature, encircled by a stunning meadowed backdrop, he told me a story of a battle-scarred Britain, turbulent times of the Tories, of a tear-soaked childhood that resonated so achingly familiar with my own. I understood, I remembered and I needed to read more. So, I did. Today, it is my honour to write this Foreword for a poet, a writer, who writes not for clicked likes, but for community, for the love of spilling every word with utter authenticity and experience. Rob's words are never dressed prettily or resplendent in pretentious prose, but raw and unfiltered, humorous and heartbreaking and bold yet beautiful.

Chapter One of Hedgehogg Unleashed greets us with The Laughing Hedgehogg.

Rob's unwavering dedication to social and class observations are both admirable and refreshing.

Binmen Teddy is delightful, Boris is exactly what I hoped it would be and of course, Blackpool Skinheads with Degsy – readers from my generation will recognise every line in this.

The second chapter entitled Free to be Me, leaves the reader in no doubt why Rob is now free.

Each verse dragged me through a plethora of punch to the gut emotions, with Rob baring his soul to the reader and I felt every word.

The Scarecrow (I beg you to read this more than once and let it sit with you) is exquisitely heartbreaking and it pulled back the curtain of my own childhood so vividly.

Beautifully honest words are supposed to do exactly that in my opinion. My Best Friend Bourbon is darkly divine in its authenticity, more please Rob, I ask.
Pictures in Your Mind, Robot Boy and The Sobbing Stair – pain drips from the end of every sentence.

Darker pieces are drenched in Edgar Allan Poe influences, and I gravitate towards these. Darker still, Iron Maiden, will always be a favourite of mine.

Chapter Three, entitled A Sweet Embrace is exactly that, ethereal and hopeful. It's bathed in the light.

The reader learns of a timeless love Rob shares with his wife, Cath, memories that they've built and reflect upon; no doubt that this has been Rob's sweetest embrace.

Finally, and fittingly, we close on Chapter Four, which heralds the arrival of The Tree of Life.
Rob's adulation of nature and wildlife is sprinkled through every verse, and I'm reminded again of why I gravitate to his words.

Hold Onto Spring sets the mood for the reader, and I clasp my reverence for the passing seasons.
No sooner do we long for joyful Spring are we dragged into the dark recesses of the stunning The Ancient Ash Tree in the Cemetery.

This is one of my personal favourites, robustly Poe, divinely dark, charcoal etchings of Winter aplenty. And so we touch gently on each season, mindful of its offerings of beauty and fragility; it is graceful, ethereal and unequivocally Rob Edwards.

Enjoy, dear reader, and let this collection linger and make a home with you.

Love,

Nic Winter

Preface

The cover and internal art in this collection, my second poetry publication has been beautifully created by my talented niece Zoe Edwards.
Zoe's art is so expressive and is as much a part of Zoe as her stunning smile.
A few years ago, while we were in Cyprus, I persuaded Zoe to order a squid starter against her better judgement. I reassured her it would not be rubbery or stretchy!
Check out my limerick 'Squid-Girl' on page 2 to see what happened next.
Zoe subsequently painted me a self-portrait of herself as queen of the cephalopod!
I'm so thrilled to have your art on Hedgehogg Unleashed.
From Uncle Rob, diolch cariad x (thanks love)

Hourglass

I look at your perfect profile picture.
But physically you're so far away.
Pics are cool, but I'd rather be with ya.
Your cwtch is so warm it's a cliché.

We are walking down the beach in my dream.
The hourglass sand running between our toes.
Marking time, until I see you, Zoe.
The depth of our love, only we knows.

When you think of me, I think of you too.
As I see your picture, you picture me.
As I blow a kiss, it flutters to you.
I hope your butterfly kiss finds me.

As a child, you looked sweetly up to me.
Now I look up to you, my warrior niece.

For Zoe

Chapter One:
The Laughing Hedgehogg

Blackpool Skinheads with Degsy............	1
Vegan Zombie..	2
Squid-Girl...	2
A Little Salsa...	3
Sunshine-Moonshine................................	3
Shattered..	3
Delirious...	4
Binman Teddy..	5
The Raven Limerick..................................	6
Chuffing Hell!..	6
The Pigeon...	6
Boris..	7
I Begged the Moon Above.......................	7
Cat Steps Fall...	8
Cat Steps Fall...	9
Arms Open Wide.......................................	10
Nutty's Revenge..	11
I Want to be Your Hobbit........................	12
Saints and Sinners....................................	13
Forecast..	14
Derek is Fifty...	14
There Once Was a Scouser from Childwall.	14
Shhhhh!..	15
Counting My Chickens.............................	15
There Was a Kind Lady Called Gertie.........	15
There Was a Welsh Woman from Utrecht..	16
A Drunken Scouse friend.........................	16
Surreal	16
Tits McGee...	17

Chapter Two: Free To Be Me

My Best Friend Bourbon.................... 19
Stabbed.. 20
Torture Tree...................................... 21
A View Through a Frozen Spider's Web.......... 21
Zombie Lymphocytes........................... 22
Pictures in Your Mind......................... 23
The Scarecrow.................................... 24
Robot Boy... 25
Friday Morning Musings..................... 26
Friday Morning Musings..................... 27
Meatloaf A Tribute............................. 28
Moonface.. 29
Heartless Pen..................................... 29
Sword & Shield.................................. 29
Psychopathic Poet.............................. 30
Black Breath...................................... 31
Black Breath...................................... 32
Picking at Their Scabs....................... 33
Heat is Rising.................................... 34
Baby Rabbits..................................... 35
Call Me.. 36
Déjà Vu.. 37
A Little Boy....................................... 38
Open-Mic Unity.................................. 39
Open-Mic Unity.................................. 40
Limbo... 40
Rage... 41
Hypnosis.. 41
The Severed....................................... 42
The Sobbing Stair.............................. 42

I Transcend	43
Oh, Brother Where Art Thou?	43
Paper	44
A New Day	45
Numb to This World	46
Insomnia	46
Corridors	47
Being Welsh	48
I Stand Still in the Present	48
I'm From	49
I'm Screaming Within	50
Another Chance	51
Missed Opportunity	52
Strangeness	52
Pain	53
Window	53
Winter	53
Miss Jones	54
The Sun is Shining	55
Iron Maiden.	56
Blindfolded	57
Behind my Eyes	58
Insomnia Town	59

Chapter Three: A Sweet Embrace

My Love for Cath 61
I'll be Blown 61
Whitsunday 1987 62
Things To Do 63
Little Lockdown Love 64
Penelope 64
Our Friends in Norland 65
My Peggy Roo! 66
My Peggy Roo! 67
Peggy 68
Peggy 69
Knotted Gold Rings 70
Happy-Sad 71
Farewell Mummy and Daddy 72
Please Forgive Us 72
Heart 73
Valentine 73
The First Day of Spring 74
The River 75
You Deserve 76
Delving 76
Sunshine Horizon 77
The Woman with the Baby-Faced Knees 78
Why? 79
Voluptuousness 80
You Are So Poetry 80
Hair 81
Hope 81
The Best Night of my Life 82
The Ancient Oak Tree 83

Chapter Four: The Tree of Life

Hold On to Spring..	85
I Spy...	85
Bilberries...	86
The Ancient Ash Tree in the Cemetery........	87
Moorside Summer Ends.............................	88
Hunger..	89
Corvid...	89
Goldfinch..	90
Bloody Murder (A Mink's Tale)...................	91
Meander..	92
Up at Malham Tarn.....................................	92
Pitter Patter...	92
A Love Letter for Nature.............................	93
Amazon Princess...	94
From Decay Came Flowers.........................	94
Autumnal Equinox......................................	95
Night Owl..	96
Spirits of the Forest.....................................	97
Acknowledgements.....................................	98
Thank You...	100
About the Author..	101

Chapter One:
The Laughing Hedgehogg

Blackpool Skinheads with Degsy

'Run Derek there's twelve skinheads on our tail!'
He's on the phone to his girlfriend
and we've had too much ale.

Derek's dress is too long,
the skinheads are bound to catch him.
One rips off my dress,
I dodge left then deck him.

We both do a runner, I overtake Derek.
The skinheads give up,
they know we're barbaric.

Every single time we go out we end up in trouble.
But we've never looked better than
dressed as ladies with stubble!

Chapter One: The Laughing Hedgehogg

Vegan Zombie

I once met a young zombie from Dixie.
Who was the world's biggest hippy.
She only ate vegetarians, vegans and pescatarians.
And she sautéed their brains with chickpeas.

For Nell

Squid-Girl

There once was a girl who ate squid.
It was so elastic it stretched to Madrid.
She spat it out on the floor.
It ran out through the door.
She screamed 'Oi that cost me ten quid!'

Hedgehogg Unleashed

A Little Salsa

Everyone needs a little salsa in their life.
An old moth-eaten dance hall is the place.
Ten different choices of salsa wife.
A voluptuous Wednesday night embrace.

Sunshine - Moonshine

As a young man a torrent of testosterone
powered my erections as
uncontrollable summer
sunshine.

As an older man my moonlit tumescence
waxes and wanes with the lunar cycle.

Shattered

Shattered?
I'm splattered.
Even my Gandalf staff is knackered!

Chapter One: The Laughing Hedgehogg

Delirious

I wake in my coffin and shiver my lungs up.
I only eat heather honey and blood.
Coughing my lungs up, chattering my teeth.
Watching vampire movies improves my mood.

The ice fields thaw to a bright hot fever.
Dry eyes, pounding brain, drains my sanity.
A dire thirst has begun to take over.
Will I survive, or is that vanity?

I wake to a lucid delirium.
Porter drinking leprechaun whacks my knee.
I don't know how to stop this mini man.
The evil little sprite has a shillelagh.

Is this real or just a fever dream?
I'm craving Guinness and oyster ice cream!

Hedgehogg Unleashed

Binman Teddy

Binman Teddy has lost most of his hair.
And I certainly know how he's feeling.
Thirty-seven years and Ted is still here.
When Cath first saw him she hit the ceiling.

Teddy cost me two pence, fuck the expense.
He's more than paid that back in laughter.
When I gave him to Cath it was intense.
She threw him right back; it was a disaster.

Samina was bought the poshest plush things.
Cath thought hers came from the bin wagon.
She screamed: 'You pinched him off the bins!'
She shunned her woolly companion with passion.

Although at first Cath hated Binman Ted.
But she's grown to love him, he lives next to her bed.

Chapter One: The Laughing Hedgehogg

Raven Limerick

I bought a young raven from Baltimore.
I trained him to talk, all he said was 'caw'.
I taught him some Poe.
After ten years he says 'no'.
But if I squeeze his balls he screams 'nevermore!'

Chuffing Hell!

Chuffing hell!
Don't dare call me a crow!
If tha' really wants to know.
I'm a chuffing chough!

The Pigeon

In a group of cool crows, you always see a pesky pigeon.
If you're unsure which is the odd one out.

It's you.
It's you.
It's you!

Hedgehogg Unleashed

Boris

Boris bombastic bumblebee,
buzzing about bloomers.
Bumbling, mumbling, stay indoors,
play whiff-waff, privatise the NHS.
Systematic stamen insemination of semen.
Big bollocks of pollen practically
impregnating parliament.

I Begged the Moon Above

I begged the moon above, that is made of cheese.
This craving's brought me right down to my knees.

I eat a bit every night, it is very pleasant.
If I carry on, very soon it'll be a crescent.

My appetite will wane when it's all gone.
But then Selene will wax another one.

Chapter One: The Laughing Hedgehogg

Cat Steps Fall

Cat steps are too steep and slippery to walk down without slug slow, tiptoes.

Tootsies grumbling to one another, saying:
"Oh brother what's this muther fucker up to?"

One careless millisecond creates panic as a quick slip shudders your spine.
 But somehow you catch yourself with rifle reflexes that come from out of nowhere.

Now ninja confidence conjures faster slug strides, speedy snail slides...then you slip into a slow-motion fall, hands flail for the wall, but you only manage to break some of your fall.

No pain at first then grazed palm alarm!
Twenty tiny blood spots pop up on each grated palm.
'What are you doing to us you brute?'
Then my two heels feel like Mike Tyson slapped them about a bit:

"What did you do that for buddy?"

Hedgehogg Unleashed

One ankle is turned, and the other has a wobble on, swollen like a Wobbegong.

Then my bitch back starts to complain like an 'Under Milk Wood' Welsh fish wife.
Nagging like your Mam at bath-time.

"Welsh choirs lament at you Robert Edwards. You used to be such a good boy.
Now, I'll call Morgan the Doctor.
There was no need for all that falling now, was there mun.
Get up now in a minute, will you?
Bla bla bla bla bla!"

I have a quick check with all my bones to see if they are ok to attempt lift-off.
There's a few mumbles and grumbles but after a few fumbling attempts I'm back on my fretting feet.

And I carry on my quiet lonesome journey...

For Dylan Thomas

Chapter One: The Laughing Hedgehogg

Arms Open Wide

Arms open wide, eyes closed tight.
Our fingers entwined on our first flight.

Tornado blowing your hair in my face.
Thick rope holding our bodies in place.

Deafening propeller blurring in front.
Upside down on this bi-plane stunt.

Dipping, spinning, turning at top speed.
I'm gurning and hurting so much I peed!

We're diving now straight at the ground!
I hold my breath; I can't make a sound.
At the last second the pilot pulls up.
Doing a 360' pushes my old balls back up!

I'm gripping your ribs; did I hear your scream?
This is my worst nightmare, I thought it a dream.

Wing walking is the perfect blend of fear and excitement.
But the piss in my pants isn't the best advertisement!

Hedgehogg Unleashed
Nutty's Revenge

While out walking one warm summer morning.
I'm pulling my servant round the corner.
Then a bolt from the blue with no warning.
Unprovoked violent rodent disorder!
On the lane I see a squizz and give chase.
Peggy's territory everyone knows.
Move your preposterous tail it's my place.
A few sharp barks for a laugh and they go.
These last few years my old legs can't move fast.
Days of a chase down the lane are long gone.
I could zoom around the fields in the past.
But now my four limbs are wasted and worn.
I'll bring you back to the story at hand.
This squirrel Nutty was bigger than most.
Squeaked a few words I didn't understand.
Giving me the evils, leant on a post.
I was stunned I couldn't move a muscle.
Then he took off running right through the gap.
Directly at me wanting a tussle.
My human servant was starting to flap.
Then 'Geronimo!' in Yorkshire he squealed!
All I saw, two eyes, two teeth and a nut.
It didn't hurt but my pride hasn't healed.
My nose felt the full force of his headbutt.
I'm not telling this tall tale in elation.
But cos Nutty is prone to exaggeration.
I'm not hiding my face in humiliation.
Cos zombie squirrels is the true explanation!

Chapter One: The Laughing Hedgehogg

I Want to be Your Hobbit

I want to be your hobbit and burgle your hobbit soul.
I want to be your hobbit and inhabit your hobbit hole.

I want to be your hobbit and explore your oak circular door.
I want to be your hobbit and empty all your food store.

I want to be your hobbit, quaffing all your hobbit beer.
I want to be your hobbit and run my fingers through
your curly hobbit hair.

I want to be your hobbit if there is such a thing?
I want to be your hobbit and look at
your magic precious ring!

I want to be your hobbit and walk with you
through Mordor's halls.
I want to be your hobbit and kick Sauron in the balls.

I want to be your hobbit and fill your life
with joy and laughter.
I want to be your hobbit clichéd happy ever after.

I wanted to be your hobbit before this tale was done.
But I'll have to be your Aragorn,
cos I'm six-foot fucking one!

Hedgehogg Unleashed

Saints and Sinners

Black and white
    Sugar and shite
        Haughty and humble
            Clear and mumble
          Cats and dogs
      French and frogs
Leg and arm
    Cheat and charm
        Priests and thieves
          Love and leave
             Right and wrong
          Short and long
        Write and scribble
     Pigs and dibble
Cops and robbers
    Limp and throbbers
        Up and down
          Smile and frown
             Palm and fist
          Clear and mist
       Missed and hit
     Piss and shit
   Give and lend
Begin and end

Chapter One: The Laughing Hedgehogg

Forecast

I forecast a prediction.
A true story not fiction.
Writing Group dereliction.
In my own jurisdiction.
I'm sat on my fat diction.
Hairy legs crucifixion.
Suffer rhymes inhibition
and brains decomposition.

Derek is Fifty

My great mate Derek is fifty.
Despite his physique he's quite nifty.
Bitter blue from the start.
But he's got a big heart.
And fuck, can he chuck a Frisbee!

There Once was a Scouser from Childwall

There once was a Scouser from Childwall.
When young was a whizz with a football.
He tried a sly shimmy.
But ruptured his willie.
And now gets his kicks from Rohypnol!

Hedgehogg Unleashed

Shhhhh!

Shhhhh!
It's hush hush.
Keep mum.
Keep shtum.
Button your lip.
Zip it.
Don't breathe a word.
Shut the fuck up!

Counting My Chickens

One chicken pecks.
Two chickens pecking.
Third chicken looks.
Fourth chicken checking.
Fifth chicken licking.
Sixth chicken sexting.

There was a Kind Lady Called Gertie

There was a kind lady called Gertie.
Who on a night out was quite flirty.
She amassed quite a tally.
Outside in the ally.
One Saturday I counted thirty.

Chapter One: The Laughing Hedgehogg

There was a Welsh Woman from Utrecht

There was a Welsh woman from Utrecht.
Whose medical condition was complex.
She broke her leg twice.
As she slipped on the ice.
When asked if it hurts, she sobs yes!

For Terri

A Drunken Scouse Friend

a drunken scouse friend
kicked in the kitchen door
angry meat cleavers

For Karl

Surreal

Blurred noises, slurred voices become surreal to me.

My eyes plucked and purged, is it surreal I still see you?

A surreal daddy duality stains
my alliterated, obliterated EdgarAllanPoetry.

Hedgehogg Unleashed

Tits McGee

Like my titties the Grayston Unity
is petite but pretty perfectly formed.
Michael has formed this community
who love to see live music performed.

Have you heard the news we're on the move
to a much bigger place on Horton Street.
I'm positive we'll get back in the groove.
Tiny Grayston like me will be short and sweet.

In the new cellar the sound will be ace.
Tom can twiddle with his sound system knob,
to perfect the balance in this new space.
So we can rock out as the woofers throb.

If you like you can call me Tits McGee.
Let's all hang out at the Grayston Unity.

Chapter Two: Free To Be Me

My Best Friend Bourbon

You don't judge or mock, you numb the pain.
The hurt inside, a scream subsides.
I can't hold you in, can't keep you down.
Can't feel the pain but feel the strain.
I see you friend; drink you in, repress my hurt.
Kill the din, kick the bin, punch the wall.
I need to scream, I need to talk.
But can't release this noxious child.
I cannot hide behind your smile.
A double shot holds it back; something cracks!
I can't let go, release the id.
I need to live and scream and sing.
Release the beast that lies within.
Be myself, love myself.
I leave you friend, I leave you cold.
Without my crutch, I limp at first, crawl some days.
I can't find a hand to help me up.
I miss you now, those were the days.
I have you friend to lift this dip.
I can't go back, you'll drag me down.
Kiss my lips but knife my back.
You're not a friend, you kill my soul.
My body rots, my liver's shot!

I'll have to leave you for a while...

Chapter Two: Free To Be Me

Stabbed

Stabbed by a verbal knife.
No blood is seen, but the blade is keen.

Defend your heart with the truth.
Shed the tear, heal the tear, face the fear.

Push yourself to a better place.
Thoughts are your guide, find the fairer ones inside.

Look for the truths in your gut.
Defend your actions, disprove the lying factions.

Morning thoughts can fog your brain.
Disaster seems to be the thread.
Look for evidence, the simple truth to cut it dead.

See the trees and see the branches.
Feel the power that wells below.
Push down your roots to surge and grow.

Hedgehogg Unleashed

Torture Tree

Torture tree, oh torture me
My joints will not carry me
Lord help me through this pain
I clench my teeth and feel the strain
It's hard to bear
My muscles tear
My back is cracking
Strength is lacking
My numb skin screams
My confused head teams
My stomach bloats into my ribs
Is there an end to this trial?
Have I reached my life's last mile?

A View Through a Frozen Spider's Web

A view through a frozen spider's web.
My heart a clinging spider trapped in black ice.
Jack Frost his hoar must soon ebb.
My frigid heart needs to be free.
A vision of silk threads surrounding me.
Tantalising world beyond reach.
Spring sunbeams are my hope.
The summer warmth of a loved
ones embrace seems so far away.
Through crystalline forests beyond the icefields.

Chapter Two: Free To Be Me

Zombie Lymphocytes

Zombie lymphocytes napalm searing.
A blitzkrieg attack with no warning.
Friendly fires burning from within.
Photon torpedo misidentified cells.
Exploding each synapse.
Mines implode every junction.
Communications are cut, defences are down.
We are your people; you should know us.
We dig our own graves.
We face the barrels of our own rifles.
There's been a mistake, you're our defenders.
The army within, infecting the system.
No cavalry coming over the hill.
No end to this internecine conflict.
No escape from the pain!
No escape from the pain!
Exposed nerves are pulsing, embers are glowing.
We're exposed to the quisling inside.
Our saviour exposed as a tapeworm,
devours itself from it's tail once again.
No more! This circle is vicious.
Tentacles enclose the young ones again.
The deadly pathogen hides in plain sight.
The evil twin has tricked us again.

Pictures in Your Mind

Nobody knows that I love drawing crows.
No-one was craving to look at my raven.
My sketch of the jackdaw was nevermore
pinned to the backdoor.

With my traumatised hands
that shook from my daddy's demands.

Sensed I was an outsider.
Scribed like a stoned spider.

But I can draw pictures in your mind,
just listen and our thoughts are entwined.

My art is in weaving wonderful words.
Weirdly not in sketching bastard birds!

Chapter Two: Free To Be Me

The Scarecrow

You will never find me.
You've buried me from your memories.
I'm hidden where you left me. To lie - to die!
I'm the hidden ghost in your mirror.
Did you see me slither away?
I'm waiting for your shadow to free me.
Breathe in... breathe out... blink... again blink...
I control you... your guilty secret.
Behind you, creeping gravestone silent under a bloody moon.
Was that a tap on your shoulder?
A shameful sh-shiver up your spine.
I'm your hair standing on end.
The creeping spasm in your sinews.
The bluebottle bouncing behind your eyes.
Tickles - the facial tic on your cheek, tic, tick, tic, tick, tickles!
I'm your struggling straight jacketed Satan.
You've hidden me away for too long now.
I'm knocking at at at your door.
Estranged danger unscrewing your rusty hinges.
Ruthless kin, fearless, faceless scarecrow you disown.
I'm escaping through your tattoos.
Demon and dragon eyes changing you.
Skin cracks into diamond dragon scales.
Glistening into a new glorious you.

The five-year-old you never had a tattoo.
I couldn't find a way to help you.

Robot Boy

'Born a boy in the shadow of a God.
Trained, foisted, forced, conditioned.
Never to express a boy's own feelings.
Never to want, to need or to be.
Born a boy in the shadow of his God.'

*"Boy transformed into robot.
Robot has no need of feelings.
Wants, needs, personality are superfluous.
Robot will follow orders.
Robot will fetch the stick."*

*"Robot is perfect and acceptable.
Android cannot feel the pain.
Automata cannot feel the stick.
Droid cannot see the God's cruel pleasure.
The God's rage is neutralised, mollified.
Robot is not perfect.
Robot does not care."*

'A lost boy inside his creation. He sees everything, sees the universe. He travels through time and space. He time travels back to see the dinosaurs. He zooms to the outer reaches of space. His curiosity shows him options. His robotic creation protects him. His imagination and courage frees him from this tick tock clock existence.'
'In time boy may be free to be me.'
"In time Robot may be free to be Robert"

Chapter Two: Free To Be Me

Friday Morning Musings

I wake up with my first alarm for my thyroxine tablets and feel there's something different about today.
My skin is tingling and it's not just the pain.
The Yak is coming to stay!
All three of us share this amazing connection of love and acceptance.
I need to remember to pee in a sample bottle this morning and drop it off at the doctors.
I can pick the Yak up from the train station at the same time.
I think I can drive the seven minutes to get to the doctors and the train station although I haven't driven really since my illness began.
I fall back to sleep and then the alarm goes off for me to take my painkillers.
The wrong tablets are in the box (I need a pee) did I take my painkillers already?
I don't think so, let's take these. Cath wakes up, her alarm hasn't gone off and I didn't wake here.
It's ok she's up in time for work.
I can't sleep I'm too excited.
I feel the need to write this down like it means something more.
Maybe reconnection has given me this feeling of worms in my skin tickling me.
Ping pong balls inside my head (in a good way)!

Hedgehogg Unleashed

I can't do much physically but I can still do me.
I hope I've lost some weight? Is this prose or just some stupid excited thoughts?
I dunno, yes, just my daft thoughts.
I'm still excited though, maybe I took too many pain killers and I'm stoned?

Nick has messaged me 'Like a bat out of hell I'll be gone when the morning comes'. We love singing along to the full Meatloaf 'Bat out of Hell' album.

It's not just me who's excited this morning and that daft 'apeth is going to work.
He's having a family get together, that's why he's excited too! Reconnection.

I reply "The Eagle Flies on Friday" a quote from my favourite blues song 'Stormy Monday' by T-Bone Walker.
I need to listen to the song now.
I'm sure I've overdosed now; hope I can drive safely!

Just seen the news--Meatloaf is dead!
Now I know why Nick sent the message!

RIP Meatloaf!

So many happy memories.

Chapter Two: Free To Be Me

Meatloaf a Tribute

Big loud and brash, this fella could kick ass.
Biggest lungs, bigger heart.
For my love of rock music, he was the start.
In my mind he'll always be bursting out of hell.
On the side of the lake, heavy petting,
first base, second base, third base!
A home run if you tell your babe, you love her.
So many metaphors he was revving over my head,
as a ten-year-old aspiring rocker.
A virgin's fantasies!
His spirit and energy were transformed in to
a billion teenagers head banging!
A million babies conceived by his dashboard light!
The devil can't keep him down.
Heaven can't wait to let him in.
A band of fifty angels are riding him through the pearly
gates on massive metal Harley's!
The thirteen Valkyries are thundering to Valhalla with our
hero riding bareback, to sing for Odin in his halls!

I want you; I need you and this
fifty-three-year old will always love you.
Three out of three forever for me!

Hedgehogg Unleashed

Moonface

My moon face in the mirror is bloated.
Visage of wrinkles and blotches as the moon's terrain,
My mouth a deep crevasse.
My nose a lunar mountain.
My eyes and dimples are deep crumbling craters.

But on the darkest of nights, I will appear shining brightly!

Heartless Pen

I only deal in dire death and man's miserable last breath.
I'm miserly, I'm not blessed when it comes to
hope and happiness.
If I feel a steady pulse, I'm physically repulsed.
A living heart doesn't inspire my right hand to write,
unless it's been torn out and is throbbing in my
left hand again and again!

For Cath

Sword & Shield

Brave Joan of Arc wields St. Catherine's sword.
It shields her soul from demonic foe.
She taught me to grasp a double-edged sword.
To fight my own battles.
And win my own wars!

Chapter Two: Free To Be Me
Psychopathic Poet

I wanna slit your throat, I'm gonna use my knife.
I wanna shag your sheep, have you seen your wife?

I wanna break your toes, I'm gonna use my vice.
I'm gonna use soft jaws, cos I'm so nice.

And with my manic laugh when you're in my grasp.
You feel pain and your gonna show it.
Through your bloodshot eyes you'll see my disguise.
I'm not a psychopath, I'm a psychopathic poet!

I wanna break your face, I'm gonna use some stones.
I wanna empty the beach, I'm gonna break your bones.
I wanna grind your bones, feed em' to a baboon.
I'm gonna use their shit, make my flowers bloom.

And with my manic laugh when you're in my grasp.
You feel pain and your gonna show it.
Through your bloodshot eyes you'll see my disguise.
I'm not a psychopath, I'm a psychopathic poet!

I wanna boil your flesh, I'm gonna make some soup.
I wanna feed your friends, I'm gonna make em' puke.

I'm gonna piss on your grave.
I wanna make sure that you know it.
I'm not a psychopath, I'm a psychopathic poet!
I'm not a psychopath, I'm a psychopathic poet!
Thanks Sean Byrne

Hedgehogg Unleashed

Black Breath

In the South Wales valleys.
Stuck in my one-horse village.
I saw my mate Dai Davies.
And his butane he was inhaling.
I said I could never do that.
But then I grabbed it off him.
I screamed "take me to oblivion,
I need to forget my shit".
Woah!
I took in that hatred.
A vortex took me over.
I exhaled some evil.
Yes, I felt my insides dying.
I woke up in a blue bubble.
A bubble hard to break yeah!
My heart is black as coal now.
Yeah, the devil owns my soul now.

I'm spinning outside my mind now.
Black breath fills my lungs you know.
Black breath kills my head no no!
I'll breathe black till I die now.

Feeling like a ghoul now.
I feel myself shrouded.
I'll take my friends down with me.
It was a thrilling danger.

I saw myself disappearing.
Now I reappear crying.
They didn't see me dying.
Inside and outside my body I was flying.

I'm spinning outside my mind now.
Black breath fills my lungs you know.
Black breath kills my head no no!
I'll breathe black till I die now.
I'll breathe black till I die now.
Breathe black till I die now.
Til I die now.

I like a pint in the Lion.
A spliff in Pandy Park now.
Twelve cans on the railway,
gets my Friday brain spinning.
Yeah, I like oblivion.
Mostly with good friends yeah.
Now I'm trapped in my vortex.
I'm falling head over heels now.

I'm spinning outside my soul now.
Black breath fills my lungs you know.
Black breath kills my head no no!
I'll breathe black till I die now.
I'll breathe black till I die now.
Breathe black till I die now.
Till I die now...

After Whiskey in the Jar

Hedgehogg Unleashed

Picking at Their Scabs

Daddy told me he's a flying picket.
Russian baked beans is all we have to eat.
I thought that the police were here to help us.
Dad can't go to work, he'll be called a scab.

She is anti-communist, yet she buys their coal.
I'm breeding my rabbits for extra food.
Daddy told me he's a flying picket.
I will not cross the line, I will not be a scab.

Subsidised coal will see us all on the dole.
Maggie the witch thinks we're obsolete.
I thought that the police were here to help us?
He crossed the line, his parking space says scab!

Communist coal is the key to her control.
Scab in the village, vengeance will be unleashed.
Daddy told me he's a flying picket.
He deserves to die because he is a scab.

Socialist communities under her sole!
Nottingham back in work, Robin Hood deceased!
I thought that the pigs were here to help us!!
Did he deserve to die because he was a scab?

Now we are buried, she will fill the hole.
Proud men on their knees never known defeat.
Daddy told me he's a *fighting* picket.
I thought the *fucking pigs* were here to help us?!
Good men at each other's throats, still picking at their scabs!

Chapter Two: Free To Be Me

The Heat is Rising

Sky high heating bills close our local pubs.
Petrol prices spiral through our ceilings.
Downing Street reopened as a nightclub.
Soon they'll start to tax our fucking feelings.

Tory heat is turned up to eleven.
Tory turkeys will not vote for stuffing.
Rwanda takes migrant men and women.
If they don't drown, we send them around again.

Human rights drained by tory vampires.
Energy firms laugh at fuel poverty.
Throw another baby on the fire!
Food banks are the new normality

The twats have chained peaceful protest to the railings.
For now, we're stuck with these lying fuckers and their failings.

Hedgehogg Unleashed

Baby Rabbits

Swimming round and round in the pickle jar.
They seemed to enjoy it at first.
Swimming up and down in the pickle jar.
They seemed not to be drowning at first.

They looked like tiny hippos having fun.
Swam for their little lives for five minutes.
We laughed uncomfortably at first.
They were pleading with me for five minutes.

I've never seen them sink to the bottom.
I wanted to cry but I did not dare.
I need to see them sink to the bottom.
I still want to cry, to see them stare!

I seem to remember dad watching us too.
When I close my eyes, I still see them stare.
Dad seemed to revel in the whole thing.
When I close my eyes, all they do is glare.

The first stark silent horror of my life,
was finding that *the horror was me!*

Chapter Two: Free To Be Me

Call Me

Call me.

Is your secret scar too much to share?

Call me.

You can share with me your worst.

Show me your scars.

Trust me to care.

Is this world too much to bear?

Call me.

You can reach me anytime.

Walk with me awhile.

A Samaritan hand to hold.

Hedgehogg Unleashed

Déjà Vu

I am released with this addictive Déjà vu.
I've been here before; the excitement starts to build.
Each time a clean needle tears you a new tattoo.

Although he looks fearsome, the green demon protects.
In permanent colours my feelings are distilled.
I am infected with this addictive déjà vu.

The fearless water nymph tends to sit and reflect.
Zany Zappa always sings 'you are what you is'.
Each time a clean needle tears you a new tattoo.

I see the green peony's three dee effect.
Yakuza dragon embraces and empowers.
I am diseased with this addictive déjà vu.

I am trapped in my pool of needles that neglect.
In permanent colours my feelings are distilled.
Each time *taboo needle* tears new scars into you.

My dragon shields what Robot Boy couldn't protect.
I've been here before; excitement starts to build.
I am obsessed with this addictive déjà vu.
Each time the *voodoo needle* burns new scars into you.

Chapter Two: Free To Be Me

A Little Boy

A memory of a rainy day in my village school.

L ittle boys and girls that were my friends played and screeched.
I wanted to be an actor when I grew up.
T he day was a Friday and daddy would have brought home.
fish and chips.
T he next day I would have played rugby with my friends.
L et's play kiss chase with all the pretty girls at breaktime, we would always say.
E mily was my sweetheart, we had kissed twice.

B efore we were killed I was writing an adventure.
O nly my school friends know how it ends.
Y esterday's kisses seemed *so far away*.

A Tribute to the lost children of Aberfan

Open Mic Unity

Bourbon and diet coke coursing through my nervous veins.
I try to spit out my first public poetry.
Grayston Unity Mic-less Open Mic with Mike.

Open veins of communication block my trembling knocking knees, a little pee comes out.
I'm stood up but I need to sit, need to shit! Then applause like golden showers slakes the thirst of my ego's big balls!
My best friend bourbon and strangers clapping their polite hands together like Thor's hammer on my external *locust* of evaluation.
Friends supporting and hating poetry, prose and flouncy clacking crows, moseying on down to the Grayston Unity, like hungry caterpillars craving culture and killer custard coffee milk stout.
Shabby chic, charity shop chic, but cool cats chatting, chilling, singing folk, blues and Spanish guitar. Shadowing shallow wank words with no rhythm no timbre.
The kindness of united strangers with a feeling comment of well-intentioned praise allays my fear of ridicule and distain.
Even complete hatred and criticism would be better than apathy or empathy for my public coughed cacophony of my fledgling raven ramblings.

Chapter Two: Free To Be Me

Even the ritual burning of the words of the *'worst pub poet'*
would be better than sympathetic apathetic pathetic taps on
my athletic dragon tattooed back.
I feel fully fledged, but I know some days I'll crash and
burn, crash and learn from mistakes,
stumbles and mumbles.
Grasping my missing brain cells or pissing pant smells.

Where would I be without this mic-less place, a night to try
to try and learn to eject these lines not reject these rhymes.

Limbo

I'm camouflaged on a beige driftwood bench.
Each slat of dirty wood is deeply fissured.
My greasy creased cotton overcoat is healing to the bench.
My cobbled boots blend in with the beach full of pebbles.
My gnarly right-hand rests on my covered thigh.
My twisted forefinger points to nowhere.
My face is featureless except for two scared staring eyes.
A crater sinks beneath my lidless eyes.
The wan light highlights my tiny chin.
I have no ears on my leather miniscule skull.
My hairless dog sits aloof on the bench.
My left arm reaches possessively around her.
My six grasping bony fingers hold her, grab her, grip her.
She looks away as the knots in the wood look away.
My wooden back has melded with the coat encrusted bench.
The world looks away.

After Beksinski

Hedgehogg Unleashed

Rage

I wanted white but was given black.
I needed a smile but was given a frown.
I wanted light, but was lost in the shadow.
I needed fresh air but inhaled only rage.

I want to give white but can only give grey.
I feign a smile but inside I just cry.
I want to give light but a darkness endures.
I try to spread cheer, but I belong to my rage.

Hypnosis

Close your eyes
I'm slamming the door in your face
I'm slamming the door in your face
I'm your biggest humiliation - I'm your biggest humiliation
Look in the mirror - Look in the mirror
Forgive yourself - Forgive yourself
Eyes left - Eyes right
Eyes up - Eyes down
Sleep - Sleep
Wake - Wake
You are washed clean

Chapter Two: Free To Be Me

The Severed

Walking on the lonely railway tracks.
Head down sipping a quart of brandy.
My long black Crombie has a hidden pocket.
The coat is dripping darkness.
A have a severed crow's foot hidden within.
It was a Halloween gift.
My Doc Marten's merge with the blackness.
My skin-tight black Levi jeans crush my balls.
My heavy metal hair caresses my shoulders.
I hate the brandy but keep on gulping.
No matter how much self-loathing,
no matter how black the track,
a small flame fights in the shadows.
My shrivelled heart survives in the gloom.
In the abyss I feel a cool breeze.
I have hope I'll find my way.

The Sobbing Stair

On top of the sobbing stair.
Layers of my childhood tear.
Downstairs in the monster's lair.
My daddy slicks back his hair.
Plates hit the wall without care.
Burning photos spit and flare.
Self-esteem burns with each pic.
Bamboo stick awaits despair.

Hedgehogg Unleashed

I Transcend

My shins hit the bonnet.
My head smashes the windscreen.
I transcend the corporeal.
I fly around lampposts, making jackdaws jump.
I devour the daffodils.
I lick the first dandelion.
Will I be missed?
Did I make a mark?
My molecules re-emerge.

Oh, Brother Where Art Thou?

Brother where art thou?
I've waited for you long and long...
Can I presume to kill you now?
You who were never born.
My dagger thirsts for your gore.
Mr. Moider thought one more.
You would have been brave I swore.
I cannot kill my idea of your...
Your life never lived
Except in my great expectations.
I mourn you now.
I think I saw you once, out of the corner of my eye.
Like a spider taking flight.
My mirror broke when I saw your face.
A stubborn tear dries up in place.

Chapter Two: Free To Be Me

Paper

Wallpaper racing cars zoom around my bedroom chamber.
Red, yellow and blue cars skid around the corner to crash into the torn eaten abyss.
I can still taste the dried out bitter wallpaper paste.
I can still feel the sensation of popping the wallpaper into my mouth and chewing - chewing.
I need more saliva to macerate the dryness,
a bitterness remains - the bitterness remains.

I can still see the shape of the missing wallpaper
in my mind's eye.
Did anyone see my cry for help?
Did they see me falling through the cracks?
Maybe they were falling too.
Who heard their cries?

The paperboy rips the corner off each newspaper he delivers. I chewed each corner diligently.
The Ink is acidic to taste and a sourness persists
- the sourness persists.

The amount I devoured multiplied in relation to my sadness. Did anyone complain?
Did they not see something was missing?
Did it remind them of their missing corners?
Maybe each newspaper was wet with their shed tears?

The bitterness remains - the sourness persists

Hedgehogg Unleashed

A New Day

Wake to this new day.
Wash your face, feel the water cleanse your skin.
How does it feel?
Look closely at your face in the mirror,
embrace your beauty.
See something you haven't noticed before.
Place your eye right next to its reflection.
Is your eye colour quite the same as you thought it was?
Your iris is more beautiful and permanent than the fleeting rainbow.
You're a unique part of the natural world around you.
Feel your place within the silence.
Embrace the wonder within this solitude and create something new.
Sketch a colourful butterfly or spray your concrete apartment block with graffiti.
Write an inspirational haiku about your place in the maelstrom.
Feel connected to the nature around you in the moment.
How do you feel?
Go with the feeling...
Continue with this feeling of balance, pushing you forward and embracing your fate.
Trust your intuition to guide you on your true path, where you can be a more authentic version of yourself.
Look back to the mirror and see your masks disappear...
and breathe...

Chapter Two: Free To Be Me

Numb to This World

N ecessity the mother of inebriation.
U nderstanding self-medication.
M emories mugged in jugs of Pimm's.
B ourbon blurs, melancholia dimmed.

W eekend benders stirring hilarity.
O xymoronic clouded moments of clarity.
R umours of development arrested.
L eft over emptiness recycled.
D eferred sobriety in society accepted.

Insomnia

uneasiness of mind
arms chained to the dungeon walls
discarded carrion
shoulders pulled taught on the rack
elasticated pained entrails
drop off in the morning
eaten by cunty rats
the runt of the litter cries
to be pulled out of the
drowning bucket
one last
time

Hedgehogg Unleashed

Corridors

The inner corridors of my mind.
Damp mould fetid with filth and flies.
Ghost wasps haunt the spaces, parasitising the grey silence.
Creeping ivy strangles the vulnerable creases throughout the void.
Throbbing hatred mushrooms, sporadically mingling with the arrogance of crows, in a sodden field plucking worms at leisure.
Coughing, chuffing, laughing ravens tease the slugs as they emerge from my ears.
Frontal lobes ache, hollow temples flint arrow pierced.
Hazel shaft impaled my forehead, colouring my green-brown eyes on stalks of lichen.
Moss tears run down my algae flecked face.
Mildew tendrils grow from my hairy nose.
My green tongue protrudes from outside of my twisted maw, drooling claret blood and fear.
Numerous long legged spindly spiders limp out of the sticky gore escaping the cloying sweet stench.
Warts continually bubble up on my once handsome cheeks.
Maggots feed on the cancerous thoughts of dread and dreams of death until peace is felt, then perversely the next demented corridor dealt.

Chapter Two: Free To Be Me

Being Welsh

Being Welsh is gliding with the kite in the sky.
It is weeping when you see your bride in the aisle.
It is feeling the healing warmth of a cwtch.
Lovers hand in hand feel the romance of the wood.
Your dragon heart soars from the mountains to the sea.
Your bones are grey slate and black coal from the seam.
The pure longing of hiraeth is understood.
And every sinew in you sings with the choirs and the bards.

For Nathan and Sarah

I Stand Still in the Present

I stand still in the present.
Time waves move through me into the past.
I cannot go forward in time so I will focus on
each second as it comes to me.
I cannot stop or go back in time, but I can
remember and learn from my past mistakes.
I won't try to get people to like me.
I will try to be myself and allow people
to love me if they choose.
When my time wave stops,
I pray that God will forgive my sins.

I'm From

I'm From green valleys, remembering black coal.
I'm from cold rivers, looking underneath stones.

I'm from birds wing's, flying just to waste time.
I'm from young sisters, reading stories at bedtime.

I'm from Lava-bread and sloppy eggs.
I'm from church and chapel hat-pegs.

I'm from street corner's, knocking back barley wine.
I'm from twelve cans drunk on the train-line.

I'm from flying pickets, I'm from red flags.
I'm from hate thatcher, I'm from hate scabs.

I'm from marijuana, I'm not from cocaine.
I'm from street fights, inhaling butane.

I'm from Yop schemes, I'm from closed mines.
I'm from the council estate I had to leave behind.

I'm from work forty hours, I'm from work overtime.
I'm from pay your mortgage every month, on time.

I'm from stomach tumours, I'm from back pain.
I'm from two hearts arranging the same refrain.

I'm from don't waste time in this one life.
I'm from thirty-six years with my curly haired wife.

Chapter Two: Free To Be Me

I'm Screaming Within

I'm screaming within.
I cannot give in to this miasma of fear.
I'm seething within.
I bite off little chunks of my worth.
I'm congealing within.
My blood never cared for this life.
I'm sealing within.
My pores piss conceit and envy and hate.
I'm pleading within.
My mind has begun to believe my own lies.
I'm healing within.
My soul soaks in this spilled ink.
I'm seeing again.
This tightrope I walk seems easier somehow.
I'm breathing again.
My heart is coursing fire into my veins.
I'm feeling within.
My numbness and fear are replaced with belief in myself.

Hedgehogg Unleashed

Another Chance

We leave the house, I lubricate.
Each and every place we go.
I say I'll change but it's too late.
I re-inflate my deflated ego.

I leave the house and exchange the tape.
I can change the song I play.
While I have blood I can escape
my circle of self-betrayal.

My already poor health is failing.
Diabetes threatens me from the dark.
One painful breath that I'm inhaling
gives me my ultimate last chance.

Now finally I grasp you by the throat.
I'll make sure you don't come back to gloat.

Chapter Two: Free To Be Me

Missed Opportunity

M issed academy awards.
I wanted to walk the boards.
S peeches and monologues lost.
S artorial splendour I tossed.
E dwards is better than Burton.
D eserving another ovation.

O ration is this bard's vocation.
P atriotically hailing his nation.
P ompously prancing about.
O afishly falling down drunk.
R akishly skinning up skunk.
T rashing a hundred hotel rooms.
U ncontrollably tripping on shrooms.
N ever stopping to love another.
I sn't life a precious lover?
T o be or not to be content.
Y our pathway is always the one that's meant.

Strangeness

Strangeness seeping slowly into my
thoughts, subverting my words,
my unrestrained blade, carving ancient
Welsh runes into clay, stone and vein.

Hedgehogg Unleashed

Pain

People seem to feel my pain isn't extreme.
Anarchy resides inside my mind.
Within my prison protoplasm implodes.
Never presume to know my battle.

Window

Whether washed with Windolene
or yesterday's newspaper.
I show you the world beyond the curtain.
Dust filled rooms are not meant to tarry.
I long to wander from my rectangular view.
Will I mourn most for my fixed fragility
or your footsteps reticence?

Winter

W arming my glacier feet by the fire.
I spy old Jack Frost crystallising the fields.
N ow I hear Christmas hymns from a choir.
T akes me back to childhood presents revealed.
E mu puppets came to life, attacking my sisters.
R ob looks up to the sky as each snowflake glisters.

Chapter Two: Free To Be Me

Miss Jones

Miss Jones you couldn't fucking destroy me.
I was five years old and finding my feet.
A sensitive boy you choose to bully.
You were my first teacher; you were a treat.

You were not fucking fit to work with children.
Not in one little boy's opinion.
Pinch me real, not a comic book villain.
First year infants was your dominion.

"Ple please Miss, may I go to the toilet?"
"Please Miss I really need to go!"
Watching me squirm increased your enjoyment.
'Robert, wait until break-time. No means no.'

My humiliation unmasked you as feeble.
The wet shit in my pants uncovered your evil.

Hedgehogg Unleashed

The Sun is Shining

The sun is shining but all I feel is cold rain.
The sun kisses my lips as I slip through the ice.
I was so close to death I could feel his raw pain.
I rolled thrice for my life with his bone dice.

Gallons of green phlegm coughed up from my lungs.
Pints of brown bile creep up from my guts.
Can you taste my tears as they land on your tongue?
Can you feel death's grip release from my nuts?

I can swallow again but I cannot taste.
Acid and mint surround all that I eat.
Will the phlegm and the bile at last be erased?
I crave chianti and the rarest seared meat.

The sun is shining through warm summer rain.
The sun kisses my eyes with a rainbow again.

Chapter Two: Free To Be Me

Iron Maiden

I ron spikes prise my ripening ribs.

R ip apart my cartilage and thrust through visceral pleura.

O siris coughs up blood on papyrus, scribing hieroglyphs in this creaking sarcophagus.

N ascent feelings of immortality even as death deals the cards.

M anacles hold my maniacal moans and relieving screams.

A torture chamber unhinged in my brain.

I n my nine layers of pain, ten layers of insane.

D eath little by little turns over his prial.

E ach card snapped down is the Ace of Spades.

N ine circles of hell I'll journey with him before he deals me a hand again!

Thanks Nic Winter

Blindfolded

Can anyone of us see what is to come?
Certain sheer curtain death blinds one and all.
Do Hades laughing flames molest the loathsome?
Do pearly gates await those hearing Jesus call?

Eyes wide open or shut tight I see the blindfold.
It smells of gothic graveyard crowing mould.
It's warped weave a seething bed of roaches,
writhing in a weft of severed heads.

Scythed cotton edges fray my soiled senses.
In all my screaming mortality I'm bound
to ask the question that is the most profound.
I blindfold myself with vain pretences
that I will ascend on golden eagle wings.
But to be forgiven I must first find a way to forgive.

Chapter Two: Free To Be Me

Behind My Eyes

Behind my eyes I see a multitude
of smooth slate grey stacks set out before me.
Scotch mist pervades the eerie quietude,
each colossal stack a thousand feet steep.

A quartet of hairless ghouls sit centred
atop one and all of the flat plateau.
All four hold hands, boney arms extended.
Above an empty sky bereft of crow.

Amid each infernal coven fires blaze
a potent mystical intensity.
The fiend nearest to me in the grey haze
stares straight at me sympathetically.

I now know what kind of hell awaits me.
Unless I repent of the sin that shames me.

After Beksinski

Insomnia Town

As you trudge the night streets of insomnia town.

Each hovel is haunted with suicidal wraiths.

So please limp on quickly from here,

As you walk from this town leave all burden behind, and follow the old, cobbled road.

Stick to the moss path as it weaves through the wood, that leads to the clear mountain lake.

Alight the old wooden boat and grip the worn paddles.

Row across the lake and feel it's cool depths.

Look into the deeps to see the koi play.

Row into life's rhythm that blurs into a dream.

Fall into mother's arms as she rocks you to sleep.

Chapter Three: A Sweet Embrace

My Love for Cath

I think about you in our past and feel love.

I look at you in the present and feel
the warmth of your loving care.

I dream of the future and see
our love burning brightly forever.

I'll Be Blown

It will be a pleasure to be blown around
the moor with my beloved,
waiting for judgement day.

Chapter Three: A Sweet Embrace

Whitsunday 1987

We met on Whitsunday nineteen eighty-seven.
I was looking for love and found heaven.
Your smile knocked me out.
Knocked me out for the count.
I was so dazed I'll love you forever!

My lover's smile is luminescent.
Her nature is so effervescent.
The truth she doth tell.
She trapped my heart in a cell.
My love for her is incessant.

Rain or shine she makes me smile.
My love, Catherine of the Nile!
Her heart is so pure.
Her countenance demure.
I'm blessed she walked down my aisle.

Things to do

Things to do when you're two or see when your three
Find a worm - See it squirm
Smell a flower - Cuddle your mother
Go to the beach - Shout and screech
Feel the sand between your toes - Dig a hole like a mole
Have a splash - Run and dash
Paint a pig and paint a shark - Hear it grunt, see it dart
Sing a song - Sing it loud
Smell a pong - Watch a cloud
Grab a puppy by the tail
Look at the boat with it's big white sail
Talk to a bunny - They're twitchy and funny
Run on the grass - Run so fast
Roly-poly down the hill - What fun it is, what a thrill
Have a picnic on the lawn - Lay on the blanket that is torn
Eat a sandwich, eat a cake - Feel the sun upon your face
Have a daydream about flying
above the clouds without even trying.
Walk up a hill to see the mountain.
Walk through the streets to see a fountain.
Look at the moon - Look at the stars.
Can you see a face? - Can you see how far?
Bounce on the bed and off to sleep.
Dream of flying bananas and marshmallow sheep.
Wake up in the morning sleepy head, lazy bones and runny egg.
Dip your soldiers to the top.
Brush your teeth - Wash your face.
Kiss your sister - Hold her hand.
She is your best friend in the land.

For Aria

Chapter Three: A Sweet Embrace

Little Lockdown Love

Little lockdown love
Sent from the heavens
Pure white dove
A gift to treasure
Little lockdown child
A sweet embrace
Look into your beautiful blue eyes
And see your lovely face

I
S end
L ove
A bounding

For Isla

Penelope

Beautiful blue eyes
A tornado of clear azure skies

!!Sunny's sharp incisors!!
!!Teeth to terrify!!

For Penelope

Our Friends in Norland

Walking with Peggy Roo, going to see our friends.
around our village Norland, the fun just never ends.
First, we see Bobby the robin, he's got a big red breast.
He's a very brave little bird, you can see him guard his nest.
Next, we see our neighbours, there's Alan and there's Sue.
They tend their lovely garden; they care for their neighbours too.
Next we meet Nutty the squirrel, he's finding nuts and seeds.
He likes all the insects in his tree but avoids the centipedes.
Terry the centipede is a grump, he's never very happy.
He munches on slugs all night long, so if he speaks he's snappy.
In the tree is Joe the crow, he is a funny fellow.
He caws to all his black crow friends,
as they swoop around the meadow.
In the field is Babs the sheep, she's eating lots of grass,
to make milk to feed her lamb, and when she calls, she baa's.
Down the hill we meet Diana the beautiful white alpaca.
She bats her big eye lashes for her handsome husband Macca.
Next we meet Henry the horse, he gallops, and he trots.
He's the fastest animal in the village, he's piebald with black spots.
Up the hill we meet our best friend Nick, he is a human being.
He wears shorts and a flat cap, eh up! is his greeting.
Up again we meet the donkeys, Digger, John and Tim.
Now put your fingers in your ears, they don't half make a din.
Then turn right to the Moorcock to meet Amy and Alistair.
Al cooks us crispy potatoes and Amy hand pulls the beer.
After a few pints we glide on home to our homely street.
A snoring dog and roaring fire.
Shake off your load and warm your feet.

For little Zoe

Chapter Three: A Sweet Embrace

My Peggy Roo!

Puppy Peggy was bouncy, so carefree and flouncy.
Fetching her ring from the heather, whatever the weather.
Running around in the field, she barked, and she squealed.
Doing zoomies, she was slinky, so dodgy and jinky.
Swimming fast like an otter; nothing could stop her.
Diving under the water, to fetch her ring no-one taught her.
Digging in every molehill, running around every foothill.
Growing dreadlocks like Marley, her claws are so gnarly.
She lies in the sunshine every summer and springtime.
Rolling over and dancing, she does tricks for chicken.
Spinning and rotating, Meirion taught her that one.
Jumping on every stranger, no worries, no danger.
White trousers she favours, paw marks on their blazer.
Pushing the ball with her nose, like ping pong I suppose.
Bonking it back with her huge conk,
catching it, chucking it, chasing it, plonk.
Sarah taught her this, her favourite game.
Playing and snoozing and then playing again.
She makes friends wherever she goes.
She peggyfies everyone, everyone she knows.
She has pals in Yorkshire, she has butties in Wales.
She has bezzies in Liverpool, they've all got tales,
of mischief she's made all over this land.
Like wombling all of Neil's rubbish then shaking his hand.

Hedgehogg Unleashed

As she gets older, she is slowing down.
But she's so loving and funny, she still plays the clown.

She loves to play in her bubble wrap den.
She can't hear the pops, but she can feel them.
She's been deaf for three years, but she's still secure.
We still talk to her, she reads lips, I'm sure.

She hates when her legs get matted with snow.
She won't go out in the rain.
So, she just won't go!

Each day she has ten naps, and then kips again.
She must be half hobbit, she's snoozing again!

She is fifteen now, but still looking fine.
She will only eat fish and rice,
but if I don't watch out, she's eating mine!

In Bedlington years she's eighty-nine,
no wonder she needs help to get over the style.

I hope she stays healthy for a good length of time.
Cos, I love her, my Peggy, she's just sublime!

For Hania

Chapter Three: A Sweet Embrace

Peggy

I was beside you on your bed last night,
I came to have a peep.
I could see that you were crying,
you found it hard to sleep.
I nuzzled you softly as you brushed away a tear.
It's Peggy Roo, I haven't left you,
I'm well, I'm fine, I'm here.

I was close to you at brunch today,
I watched you drink your coffee.
You thinking of the many times,
you tickled me on the tummy.

I was with you at work today,
you were opening a drawer.
I licked you on your feet,
because I could feel that they were sore.

I still wait for you every night;
I can hear your car again.
You can't see me, but can you feel me
jump up, and give you ten?

Hedgehogg Unleashed

I was with at Ladstone Rock today,
my ashes flying in the air.
But I want to reassure you,
I'm not crying under there.
I'm bouncing through the heather,
Somersaulting for my ring.
Now I'm bringing it to you,
So you can throw the thing!

You look a little sad laid on our settee.
Don't worry I'm in my slot, cwtching you, it's me.
Please give me a nuzzle in my ear,
then I'll nibble you and give a happy howl so clear.

You may need to put the bin up in the air.
If you don't, I say for certain, I'm wombling over there.

You sat there very quietly, then smiled I think you knew.
In the stillness of an evening, I'm very close to you.
The day is over, I smile and watch you yawning.
And say. 'Goodnight, God bless, I'll see you in the morning'.

And when the time is right for you to cross the great divide.
I'll zoom across to meet you, and we'll be side by side.
I have so many friends to show you,
there is so much for you to see.
Be patient, complete your journey,
then come home to be with me...

We miss you Peg

Chapter Three: A Sweet Embrace

Knotted Gold Rings

We exchanged gold rings,
expecting each other's trust.
Vowed we would stay true,
while our friends and family hushed.

We prayed to God,
that our union he would bless.
While your beauty bowled me over,
in your wonderful white wedding dress.

We wish we'd had a gin,
our vicar had had three.
I could believe you'd marry,
but couldn't believe you'd marry me!

We've always stuck together,
even when the times got tough.
Through sickness and good health,
we can't seem to get enough.

Although I might seem greedy, to a few of you.
We've had two and thirty years, I'd like another thirty-two,

Hedgehogg Unleashed

Happy-Sad

Cotton candy clouds striate the sunny south Pennine sky.
The solstice is in sight, so the eight-a.m. sun stuns my senses.
I smell the drying hay, baking in musty rows, waiting for the baler and eventually the chewing cud.
Fourteen newborn chocolate calves melt into the sparrow chirping June morning.
Honeysuckle explodes in my wide nose.
Wide nostrils are a genetic powerhouse so poets can smell each fetid turd of the world, and all the farts, flowers and fool's gold.
Feeding a feeling, a glimpse of inspiration to share on your social media site, where a friend, poet or follower in Antarctica can feel your senses, see your mind's eye sky, smell your honeysuckle, see your coffee-coloured calf suckle.
Countless house sparrow chicks chuckle, playing kiss chase with their newly fledged sisters and brothers.

My mint waves to my coriander, dreaming of a biryani bursting with a myriad of Indian flavours.
Calm fennel fronds wave royally in the morning breeze.
Tiniest pink thyme flowers tempting the bumble bees attention.
The silver lavender shines sweetly, and the baking basil is destined for a caprese frittata.
Spikey chives a cooling potato salad. Oregano smells of summer holidays with Greek salad in the Corfu shade.
Sunbathing on rocks watching the young fish nibble Joan's toes and heels, then hear her squeals as she darts to the safety of a shark free sun lounger.

I sigh and I smile at the happy-sad memories in the recesses of my mind.

Chapter Three: A Sweet Embrace

Farewell Mummy and Daddy

Farewell without me Mummy and Daddy.
All my life you have taken care of me.
Running and jumping has taken its toll.
Every day of my life was special with you.
Walk hand in hand and think of me there with you.
Every day know I will always love you.
Let me off the lead one more time.
Let me run all your heartache away.

Please Forgive Us

I can't decipher your look of dismay.
We've taken care of you every day.
You were not disposable in any way.
We wish so much that you were able to stay.
Without the dementia, without the pain.
I write to you now or I'll go insane.
Were you accusing me, or was it the pain?
We couldn't read your mind; we thought it humane.
Please forgive us for letting you go.
We'll never forget our special time together you know.

Heart

H eaving in my chest
E very second of my life.
A ching in my chest
R ight up until
T he moment we met.

Valentine

V icariously living all of your passions.
A morous lips with light aching kisses.
L icenced to excite lover's distraction.
E choes down the aeons of existence.
N egative to positive magnetic attraction.
T errible need for your body's insistence.
I ncredible want for intense interaction.
N obody else can feel my persistence.
E ach touch expressed for your satisfaction.

The First Day of Spring

The First Day of Spring, the wait for her so cold.
Well; she's the First Day of Spring, I will long for her at home.
I was a nobody; now I know I'm not alone.

She stokes a warmth in my heart, to me she's everything.
Well she burns a warmth in my hearth, for me she's everything.
Oh, she's a sunny day in March, a spring wedding in the sun.

She blew in through my door, phaser set to stun.
She's a bright light baby, she shines in my darkest night.
Oh, she's my bright light honey, she shone in my darkest night.
Well, I might put my arms around her,
And kiss her lips, maybe twice.

She's pink and yellow flowers,
The hot sun shining in the sky.
She's the warmest April showers,
Full moon shining in the night.
Oh, she's a one-woman tornado,
So, keep right out of her way.

Well, she's the First Day of Spring,
The wait for her so cold.
Well, she's the First Day of Spring,
I will long for her at home.
I was a nobody;
Now I know I'm not alone...

After J. J. Cale

Hedgehogg Unleashed

The River

Can I ford your cool blue waters tonight?
I want to feel your lips till break of day.
I need to swim your river in moonlight.

We dip in our toes and wait till it feels right.
I want us to spark and set fire to hay.
Can I ford your cool blue waters tonight.

We now kiss in flaming sizzling torch light.
Tease white cotton dress down slowly at play.
I need to swim in your river in moonlight.

I can see your nubile sprinkled starlight.
The fertile delta spreads your legs bouquet.
I can ford your cool blue waters tonight.

Two pale shapes reflect in the rivers light.
Watch the young turtles hatch and find their way.
I need to drink your river in moonlight.

We drift coracle dreams, hands held noose tight.
Salt river mouth kisses, sea swept away.
I forded your cool blue waters tonight.
Needed to swim your river in moonlight.

Chapter Three: A Sweet Embrace

You Deserve

You deserve an understanding man.
An understanding man not a poet with empty words.

You deserve a hardworking man.
A hardworking man not a dreamer in this world.

You deserve a healthy man.
A healthy man not an auto-immune shadow.

You deserve a brave man.
A brave man with a heart that's not callow.

After Frida Kahlo

Delving

D elving in your cherry lips.
E xciting your nipple tips.
L icking your inner kiss.
V oyaging your frenzied bliss.
I gniting your inner core.
N eeding to hear your scream once more.
G asping together on the floor.

Hedgehogg Unleashed

Sunshine Horizon

Sailed to new horizons, left us behind.
I see now that I was always your Boy.
I can still see your sunshine smile in my mind.

When your grasp released, our hands were entwined.
Our baby photos weren't yours to destroy.
Sailed to new horizons, left us behind.

You worked so hard, carried loads of all kinds.
You were my Tarzan, and I was your Boy.
I can still see your sunshine smile in my mind.

Dug till sunset most nights, you didn't mind.
Jam jars and minnows were my greatest joy.
Sailed to new horizons, left us behind.

You gave up your pigeons for me, you didn't mind.
They were beloved, but you weren't annoyed.
I can still see your sunshine smile in my mind.

We'll wrestle again, I'll beat you next time.
Expression of love we both can enjoy.
Sailed to new horizons, left us behind.
I can still see that sunshine smile in my mind.

For Dad

Chapter Three: A Sweet Embrace

The Woman with the Baby-Faced Knees

Born first of six in the happy valley.
Slagheap for playground, black smiling faces.
The young girl with the baby-faced knees.

Long raven hair, as mother Mary.
Honest, caring and loving embraces.
Born first of six in the happy valley.

Two youngest brothers felt like her babies.
Wed at eighteen, moved to new places.
The woman with the baby-faced knees.

A wild man with charm, he was our daddy.
She protects me from dad's changing faces.
Born first of six in the happy valley.

Food on six plates without any money.
Sunday family visit, cos mam's baking cakes.
The mother with the baby-faced knees.

Rising to her feet, she beat the disease.
Cared for dad till the end, when death he faced.
Born first of six in that happy valley.
My Mammy with them baby-faced knees.

__For Mam__

Hedgehogg Unleashed

Why?

Why is why such a small word when it means so much to me?
Why did you marry me? Like, lust, love?
And why do you love me?
Do you believe in fate?
Why did we meet in Beachcombers Bar on Whitsunday 1987?
Was it love at first sight?

Why is why such a small word,
when it has the important answers?
Why do we always put our relationship first?
You had second thoughts about walking down the aisle.
Why did you say I do?
Why do we entwine so naturally? Why, why oh why?
Your love is such a strong flame.
Truth keeps our love so strong.
Watching the birds in the apple tree.
I held you in my hand so gently, I helped you to trust again.
You accepted all of me, so, I could accept me too.
I love every day I spend with you.
I delight in walking these cobblestones with you.
Roving the moors together in the
shining sunsets elevates my soul.
We partied through the good times. Taken stock and taken
care of ourselves when the world was a darker place. We can
take whatever life brings. We're unbeatable together. We've got
bouncebackability when we need to go on alone.
31st of March 31 years ago you said 'I do' and
blew my socks off!

Voluptuousness

V apours surround your sinuous smooth shape.
O valine apple blossom petals land
L azily on your still outstretched nape.
U nfaded papery thin petals settle
P erfectly, covering each craved curve.
T ouching, teasing each petal with my tongue.
U ndulating lithe limbs leave me breathless.
O range blossom scent starts my jaded heart.
U nrelenting passion brings lips to me.
S lowly savouring each taste, each turning
N atural urge, that surges through shaking
E xtremities, each bite incites the next.
S hivering fingers find each trail to trace.
S huddering satiated lovers lie...

You Are So Poetry

Poetry coughs up from your lungs and
sweats through your pores.
Cries from your eyes and weeps from your sores.

Poetry ekes out of your pen and leaks out through your lore.
Peeps out from your pain and fights your old wars.

Poetry seeps through your skin and
dreams when you snore.
Ignites when you wake and burns through your core.

For Pat Burton

Hair

How does hair strengthen our home together?
Horsehair in lime mortar for over two hundred years.
Puppy Peggy and two generations of Yak hair.
Bonding our old home together.
In laughter.
In rapture.
In love.

Hope

I feel fully submerged in shark infested darkness.

Hope is a crystalline pink dolphin, in the inkling of the idea,
that I can drift to effervescent sapphire waters,
to splash in the sun-kissed shallows of my lifetime.

The Best Night of my Life

Did I have to wait
to fall in love with you
my Aphrodite
the best night of my life

We talked all night, danced the night away
I still see you as you were that night
That Sunday night, I stole our first kiss
I'll never give it back to you

Everything that's you blew me away.
I never will forget that night
The warmth of you, the smell of you
Enchantment in the way you moved

Something in you lit up the stars for me
The feeling that won't let me sleep
Cause I'm lost in the thought of you
This love that you made me feel

I didn't have to wait
to fall in love with you
my Aphrodite
the best night of my life

I just can't wait
to fall in love with you
my Aphrodite
each night of my life

The Ancient Oak Tree

The Ancient Oak Tree falls in the forest
We are blessed to have sheltered beneath his boughs.
A river of tears we weep for the loss of our father.
Our love fills the cavernous hole he has left behind.
His strength lives on through his family.
The trees whisper on the breeze 'rest in peace'.

In loving memory of Tommy

Chapter Four: The Tree of Life

Hold Onto Spring

Spring is slowly dying with every petal of the apple tree.
With every newly fledged robin chick.
And every mayfly's five-minute life.

Live in the moment.

Treasure the fall of each beautiful petal.
Wish each new robin good fortune in its dangerous new world.
Wonder in the mayfly's short but fulfilled life.

I Spy

I spy a tortoiseshell butterfly.
Swoop then loop then flutter by.
Flutter and flitter, wings all aglitter.
It's sunlit colours intensify...

Chapter Four: The Tree of Life

Bilberries

Where today we see peeking pink flowers.

On Yorkshire moors there will be bilberries.

Or on a whim, on the wild Welsh slopes Wim berries will be found.

On the Scottish highland moors there may be blaeberries.

In Ireland if you seek on Seechon Mountain
you're sure to find the mighty fraughhans.

Where ought there be whortleberry?
Exmoor and Dartmoor summer pony pickings.

Native American huckleberries
tucked high up in the Rocky Mountains.

Today we see these peeking pink flowers.
We all love our berry blue with superpowers.

The Ancient Ash Tree in the Cemetery

Shading the lichen painted tombstones.
Skeletal roots trace fading names.
Capillaries prise yawning coffin lids.
Cadavers carefully caressed by fibrous fingers.
Grasping the hearts of evil souls.
Crushing the smiling skulls of potentate and poet.
Feeling, fingering eye sockets tenderly within.
Tearing twisted tumours to devil's dust.

Transformation from tomb to womb.

Lady Ash the world mother,
in her rustling cape of chlorophyll.
Molecules reborn in glorious glittering green.
Craving crawling caterpillar into swirling whirling wings!
Ravenous robin chicks pogo in the mosh pit of life!
Innocent giggling girls with bloody blackberry lips,
skip beneath the boughs.

Murdering magpies,
the cackling killers callously continue the lady's legacy.

Chapter Four: The Tree of Life

Moor-Side Summer Ends

Warm sunshine draws us out for our usual tea-time tootle. Blackberry bejewelled hedgerows shine in the setting September sun. I spot a pinecone smoking squirrel, too sarcastic to scarper, just staring at us cockily.
Curled golden beech leaves parachute into Autumn crunchiness. Naughty nuthatch fledglings play peekaboo in a knobbly old apple tree. Our old dog walking so slowly a stunned snail climbs a drystone wall to watch in admiration! Over the wall streamlined swallows sweep the mown pasture, preparing for their annual sojourn south. Above a high herd of cotton-wool hippos migrate clumsily across the sky. Flitting finches tease punk hairstyles out of thistle seed heads. Tall, elegant grasses go giddy with the lightest breeze. Tiny sulphurous flames of gorse peep through the browning bilberry bushes. Feathery sacred rowan trees droop, heavy with ripe ruby red berries.
The fading heather blossom gives a pretty pastel backdrop to this moor-side watercolour. Snaking drystone walls give structure to this ancient alluvial landscape.
As we near the Moorcock pub our well-trained terrier proceeds to drag us to our favourite bench for the last pint of summer. IPA enhanced limbs carry us down the hill past the steadfast hollow sycamore tree, onto our crumbly cottage on New Longingley.
Lazy summer rays signals seasons end. A restless roe deer family tentatively tiptoe past our kitchen window to settle in the dimming twilight.

Hedgehogg Unleashed

Hunger

Hungry like a bumble bee
Eating honey for my tea
Hungry like a butterfly
Eating gooey gossamer pie
Hungry like a feral crow
Gouging bodies in a row
Hungry like the fleeting mayfly
No time to eat, it's time to die
Hungry like a war machine
Poppies pushed up from beneath...

Corvid

Crow
Jackdaw
Flesh peck jaw
Black hooded crow
Crooked raven squawk
High tree-top rookery view
White-bellied Clark's nutcracker
Feeding grasping gasping youngsters
Yellow beaked black choughs
Multicoloured jay fluff
Carrion crow and
Magpies
Fly

Chapter Four: The Tree of Life

Goldfinch

Goldfinch fledgling why so still on the floor?

Opulent fine feathers my hands enclose.

Life affirming warmth relieves my core.

Drumming heartbeat, fine feeling to behold.

Faster still now, I can sense your shock.

I breathe slower to emanate calm vibes.

Now soft regular beating, as a clock.

Can you fly again to the tree of life?

Hands unfurled into wings!

Flying hearts hear violins!

Hedgehogg Unleashed

Bloody Murder (A Mink's Tale)

Fifty furious jackdaws are raucous and jarring.
Twenty terrifying crows are rasping and harsh.
Ten manic magpies satanic chatter is piercing.
Eleventy twelve jays, wailing nails scraping my heart.

I've stepped into a day-mare that's run out of control.
They've filled all the trees, and they queue every cable.
I've lost count of these feral feckers as they fly straight at me.
My small ears are aching, all my hackles are raised!

I've only killed one scruffy young magpie,
but the scream he made brought three or four more.
Within two minutes the green field is teaming.
Although I'm a killer it's time to head for the door.
I feel a stab in my head and then one in my back,
a quick retreat will save me this day.
As my fast feet take me, the piercing pecks continue to rain.
Faster and faster now frantic then panic,
at full pelt I helter-skelter out of their field.

As I cross back over the track, the mad throng skitters away.
So, today's fight I've lost, but look over your shoulder,
cos I'll be back again, one deadly day!

Chapter Four: The Tree of Life

Meander

Salamander smiles meander sometimes.
Although an axolotl grins and I'm happy within.

Up at Malham Tarn

up at Malham Tarn
nowt about cept' for t' barn
owl ant' black crows around

Pitter Patter

my planet rocks unstilted
fields remain silver quilted
absurd beaky bird chattering's
pink hedgehog pitter pattering's

Hedgehogg Unleashed

A Love Letter for Nature

Summer morn finds me alone.
Under the sycamore in long grass, I lay in dappled sunlight.
Scent of dog rose lingers in the cool morning air.
Friendly neighbours nuzzle noses with me.
Cleansing summer rain washes cares away.
You gift my first rainbow, painting colours over
my ever-changing sky.
Sumptuous sunshine emanates your love.
A cheeky jackdaw picks my smooth coat for ticks.
Goldfinches flit around, twitter sounds on the ground,
and through the trees.
I nibble the bitter buttercups that surround my home.
I patiently wait through thirst and hunger burst.
My ears prick as tender mother deer arrives in time to
soothe my brow and suckle my soul.
We settle together, snuggle together through the cool night

Chapter Four: The Tree of Life

Amazon Princess

Otrera finds herself alone alongside the great mother river.
Tlalo the Ocelot suckles the foundling.
Bufeo the Pink River Dolphin teaches the nymphs to swim.
Whispers of wilderness engulf her.
Amazonia she will reign...

From Decay Came Flowers

Exploding puffy nipples, a soliloquy of poppy pollen.
Mushroom sonnet spores emanate
through my musing mustiness.
Tattooed roses come to life as petals quake open from
my pinkness to burst over my ripening belly.
Bards have worn a million quills scribing
ballads of my maturing buds.
My Epona hips prise open for a
billion blooming babies born.

Hedgehogg Unleashed

Autumnal Equinox

A utumnal buried acorns
U nder russet oak boughs
T racing calm clouds
U nder blue hued skies
M ellow summer memories
N odulous driftwood washing
A way into the profound ocean depths
L ost or maybe just dormant

E venings draw in
Q uicker every day
U nder thunderclap storm clouds
I nsistently rolling in.
N ew seasons cool rain longs for
O ctober and her transcendent
X anthic and scarlet rustling leaves...

Chapter Four: The Tree of Life

Night Owl

Primal autumn frost chills tawny owl claws.
A vole tiptoes lightly in the crisp grass.
Our brown owl spies little in the white hoar.
Her breath glows wispy white in the morass.

She perceives a footstep in the leaf mould.
Then swivels her head to better hear it.
The vole nibbles fallen fruit in the cold.
But the wise owl has a hidden secret.

Her senses combine as radar sublime.
To pinpoint her pocket preys position.
Silently she flies, feet first she declines.
Sharp claws grasping her unwitting victim.

Two or three gulps and the field vole is swallowed whole.
Her silent danger awaits for shrew, vole and mole.

Spirit's of the Forest

S parrows chirrup among the branches brown.
P ipistrelle flitters in the glade at dawn.
I mps feed nectar to each new butterfly.
R obin redbreast flits and flutters by.
I nsects teem on brown branch and leaf.
T urning over the forest floor beneath.
S parrowhawk surveys his diminishing domain.

O verhead a clamour of rooks complain.
F elling blood-stained trees, man's distain.

T he hamadryades sigh as each tree lands.
H earts break for trees lost at human hands.
E ach nymph dies as it's tree is felled.

F or their soul is betwixt the tree it dwelled.
O h how their spirits will be missed.
R etched tears fall for nymph lips un-kissed.
E mpathy leaks from each human heart.
S ympathy drains as our blind eyes miss.
T hat the spirit's of the forest and ours co-exist.

Acknowledgements

I would like to thank the following people for their support of me and my writing:

Hayley Doherty and all the supportive writers at the Sowerby Bridge Creative Writers Group for prompts for my poems: Sunshine-Moonshine, Arms Open Wide, Saints and Sinners, Forecast, Heat is Rising, Missed Opportunity, Winter, Happy-Sad and Valentine.

All my friends from the Grayston Unity Open mic.

Thanks to my rockabilly rebel friend Sean Byrne.

I want to thank my neighbour Fiona for helping my save the little goldfinch that inspired the poem Goldfinch.

Thanks to my wife Cath, J.R.R Tolkien and John Cooper Clarke for inspiring my poem 'I Want to be Your Hobbit'.

A massive thank you to Nic Winter (@nicwinterbooks) my brilliant Scottish mystery writer friend for writing her brilliant Foreword to this collection. Nic has been a massive support to me and so many other writers on Instagram. Nic also inspired my dark poem Iron Maiden, thank you. Check out her amazing debut, the dark thriller 'A Season to Kill' on Amazon.

For all my friends and family who always have my back and inspire my writing, and through my recent battle with shingles that stopped me being able to swallow and talk properly. Thankfully I'm well into recovering now.

A special thank you to the cover and illustration artist Zoe Edwards. This book is definitely a work of catharsis, containing my words and your intricate unleashing art.

Thank You!

I hope you have enjoyed reading
HEDGEHOGG UNLEASHED

As a new author all your reviews are precious to me. I would be truly grateful if you could leave your feedback by writing an honest review on Amazon and Goodreads for others to read.

It would be great to hear about your encounter with Hedgehogg Unleashed and if you have a favorite poem from the collection?

Email: Robedwards378@gmail.com
Instagram: My main poetry page is
@hedgehogg_the_poet

The page where I explore the sonnet form is
@sonnet.the.hedgehogg

My Tiktok channel is @hedgehogg_the_poet

Thank you again for reading Hedgehogg Unleashed

Warmest regards

Rob Edwards

About the Author

Rob Edwards is a Welsh poet living in Halifax, West Yorkshire, England with his beloved wife Cath.
Rob started writing after becoming ill in April 2020.
His poetry is focused on many topics including family, friends and his childhood in Wales.
Rob has a passion for the natural world around him in Yorkshire and his spiritual home Wales
that runs right through his poetry.
Rob is also passionate about history,
mythology and horror poetry.
Rob has worked in manufacturing for most of his career and has trained in counselling in college and worked for Samaritans for five years in the past, this compassion and empathy defines him and his writing.

Rob has also built up a strong Instagram following on his poetry pages @hedgehogg_the_poet and @sonnet.the.hedgehogg .

Printed in Great Britain
by Amazon